Naked
in the Driveway

By Laura Brannan White

NAKED IN THE DRIVEWAY

1405 SW 6th Avenue • Ocala, Florida 34471 • Phone 352-622-1825 • Fax 352-622-1875
Website: www.atlantic-pub.com • Email: sales@atlantic-pub.com
SAN Number: 268-1250

Library of Congress Control Number: 2020908905

Printed in the United States

PROJECT MANAGER: Kassandra White
INTERIOR LAYOUT AND JACKET DESIGN: Nicole Sturk

Table of Contents

Part 2
The Appalachian Trail

Part 3
New Hampshire

I am a collector of broken hearts.
It sounds hardcore,
I know,
but all the pieces are mine.

Introduction

This is a different type of journey. It's not your manicured-toes-by-the-pool picture from your typical weekend getaway. This is more wild, bold, and, quite frankly, unhinged tale of a week-long retreat.

It's a transparent revelation of the secrets behind the selfies, similar to a page out of *Where's Waldo*—all chaotic and colorful. Except, it was peace I was looking for and not some imaginary man. Well, maybe I was looking for that, too.

The following pages contain a brief, one-week, mid-life-crisis-adventure tour told from the perspective of an overweight, divorced single mother and inner-city school teacher.

40, Satan's Numeric Bride

As a child, I remember my mother's sense of impending doom as that little, benign number steadily creeped upon her. It was with condescension at her absurdity that I watched her navigate the grip that aging had upon her life, certain that I would transcend such foolishness in my own future.

Feverishly dying her hair in the small bathroom sink felt to her like a desperate attempt to hold on to something that was being ripped away. I used to help reach the hair on the back of her neck, rubbing in the pungent dye with my bare fingers and making snide comments about how she needed to grow old gracefully. She needed to celebrate her womanhood and the aging process, not fight it.

"You will understand one day," she'd say to me.

Never, I'd say back in my head.

They say pride comes before the fall.

And now here I am, with that snide little b*tch, 40, staring me directly in the eye, like she has been waiting decades just to taunt and heckle me. All of a sudden, the measure of life's accomplishments have come into view, and it isn't just terrifying; it is painful, rage-inducing, disappointing, and so much more.

40 is Satan's numeric bride.

Here I sit in the midst of all my happily married 40-year-old friends, raising their families, arguing with their spouses over all the everyday stuff single people find petty, and wondering where it all went wrong. What did I have to show for these past four decades of my life?

The answer is a failed marriage, a rough co-parenting situation, a higher education with a lower paying career, a figure amply blessed with fullness, chronic dark circles under my eyes, and endless pieces of broken hearts—mostly mine. This life is so very far from the lofty expectations of my once-young heart. Deeply imperfect.

This is NOT what I had planned.

Naked

The rental car vents blast waves of warm air across my raw, goose-bumped skin. Shivers convulse through my entire body. My neck muscles clench in tight pulls of survival as I strain to see the road through the panicked wipers. Outside the rain rages on.

Finally, I find the small drive in the darkness, put the car in park, and my bare foot slides off the cold, rough pedal. I pick up my phone and search for the number.

I take deep breaths as I listen to the phone ring.

Finally, there is an answer.

"Umm. Hello. I know you don't know me, and this is going to sound crazy, but I am in your driveway…and I'm naked."

Like most things in my life, running away to deal with my life's disappointments didn't go as planned. If gallivanting around in all my naked glory isn't evidence enough of that, I don't know what is. I mean, I have spent my entire life avoiding tank tops and swimsuits, stating that my thighs and arms "just don't go out in public." I was too ashamed to bare the imperfect, yet far more appropriate, parts of the body, so to expose every last inappropriate area and roll certainly wasn't on the agenda for my healing process. I had simply gone searching for peace and ended up entirely exposed.

So how did I get here?

Part One
Travel Tips for a Life Crisis

Step 1: Disappear

- Go somewhere you've always wanted to go, preferably a place that would either:

    1. bore your children (if you have them) to death; or,

    2. would be inappropriate for children.

In my case, I felt as though Salem, Massachusetts, home of the infamous Salem Witch Trials, hit the nail on the head with both requirements.

- Enjoy every second of the day to the fullest. There should be no resting in the hotel room. You could do that for free at home!

- Let at least one person know that you are going off of the grid. In my case, I texted my best friend to let her know that I was going to disappear for a week and not to worry. I'd come home—eventually. I shared my location with her on my iPhone as a safety precaution only; she was under strict orders not to check it unless there was some kind of emergency.

Here's how my journey went down.

Chapter One

Day 1: Day of Disappearance

3:00 a.m. Woke up. Let's be honest, I didn't really go to bed the night before.

3:30 a.m. Arrived at the airport, and I caught a red-eye to Boston.

Two flights later...

10:00 a.m. Got rental car in Boston and drove to Salem, Massachusetts.

11:00 a.m. Checked in early to The Hawthorne Hotel.

The Hawthorne Hotel is a national historical treasure that has hosted many famous people. Robert De Niro and Jennifer Lawrence even shot some movie scenes in the ballroom here. The directors of *Bewitched* did, too, for their TV show.

If you bring along a partner on your crisis trip, which I recommend you don't, do not be cheap like me and get the "Alphonsa Boutique Style" room unless you are comfortable being completely naked in front of

(Tiny Shower)

your travel companion. The room is the size of my walk-in closet back home, and it appeared that they have converted an actual 2x2 closet into a shower. You have nowhere to step after the shower, except into the carpeted room in all of your naked glory. I originally invited a coworker to join me on this trip, but now I see it was God's providence that spared us both the trauma of such a situation.

The room itself is charming and quaint and takes you back into what feels like a simpler, classier place in time—until you find out that you are

staying in the infamous haunted room of some famous dead guy and people are constantly taking pictures of you as you exit your room.

The hotel also hands out free, unlimited water bottles at the front desk, which I utilized several times a day. Also, it has free razors, which is great because you can't take those on a plane if you only take a carry-on bag, and hairy pits (etc.) on your crisis trip is a no-no. It would just make you feel gross and dunk you deeper into the darkness.

I immediately started exploring the town and lost all track of time. This is how the day unfolded:

1. I ate at lunch at Sea Level. I tried the lobster roll and sangria.

Lobster Roll and View of Bay from Sea Level

I have to give two thumbs down on the lobster roll. The mayo defiled the essence of the fresh (and stupidly expensive) lobster. The meat was mushy and extra fishy tasting, and I almost couldn't stomach it, but at $25, I choked down every last bit. The bread was buttery, crusty, and delicious, as was the pickled coleslaw. Yum! The waitstaff was kind, quick, and professional, and the view was probably the best in Salem. But, if you go there, just don't expect to get to see the actual ocean. It is just a bay. Unfortunately, they were out of Sangria, which makes me want to give them two thumbs and a toe down. No restaurant should ever run out of Sangria. That is an essential drink for a life crisis trip.

2. After my meal, I walked to the northern tip of Salem and stared at the ferries to Boston.

3. I walked back and purchased coffee, as my lack of sleep was starting to kick in.

4. Then, I toured Nathaniel Hawthorne's birth home and the House of Seven Gables! This was the ultimate dream for my English-Language-Arts-Teacher-Nerd alter-ego.

The House of Seven Gables

Nathaniel Hawthorne's Birth Home

5. I bought myself a gift: a Scarlet Letter t-shirt with plans to proudly wear the letter, head held high as a tribute to all unfairly scorned women. I should note here that on one of these life crisis adventures, it is okay to spoil yourself.

6. I was unable to pass by the candy store on the way back to the hotel without indulging. Though I did purchase some sweets, I kept walking to burn off said indulgence.

Candy Store I Couldn't Resist   *Free Tour About Witch Trials*

8. I got in free to the Salem Witch Museum with my teacher ID. *Score!*

9. Of course, I walked some more.

Question based on my walking observations: Salem, if being a witch is about being happy and healing others, as all of your museums and tours so forcefully propose, why is this town *covered* in black paint and self-proclaimed "terrifying" witch and ghost tours? I'm confused.

10. I took advantage of my trip and toured the Salem Witch Memorial, taking pictures to jazz up my Crucible unit . (A unit is teacher lingo for a group of lessons often related to a theme or topic. In this case, one of my 10th grade units revolves around the reading and analysis of the American play, "The Crucible," by Arthur Miller. The setting of the fictional play is the Salem Witch Trials, and it incorporates characters based on the real life victims of the 1692–1693 trials.)

Commemorative Stones for Two of My Favorite Characters/Victims

11. I walked some more. At least I was going to get plenty of exercise.

12. I arrived back to the hotel to freshen up because God knows how long I had been awake and exploring at this point. I probably smelled ripe.

5:30 p.m. I ate dinner in the Hotel Tavern.

The Tavern at The Hawthorne Hotel is reasonably priced, and the food is exceptional! Plus, you get to sit in plush chairs as you sip Scarlet Letter martinis. The portobello sandwich is delectable, and the sweet potato fries were cooked to perfection. This meal alone was almost worth the trip to Salem.

The Scarlet Letter Martini

6:30 p.m. I drove to Manchester by The Sea because I figured it must be amazing since there is a movie named after it.

Manchester by the Sea appealed to me since I had recently seen the movie, but it appears impossible to see the sea in Manchester, unless you own a mansion along the shoreline. I drove up and down all kinds of streets and side roads, but I only got close to the ocean when I trespassed on a private beach in a cove.

Private beach in Manchester by the Sea

Once situated at said beach, I started a travel journal. Try it! It will make you feel like you have purpose. Plus, others will see you writing and will assume you must be important.

8:30 p.m. I abandoned my trespassing and started to journey back to the hotel. Soon I discovered my phone battery was dead, and I had no idea how to get back. Thanks to an inherently good sense of direction and ability to retrace my steps, I eventually made it to the hotel.

The next day, I decide I will head north to Rockport because I want to sit on the rocky cliffs and stare at the ocean. I'm hoping I can do that there.

That night, passing the night in my shoebox of a room, the quiet screams of my soul started to surface.

So, let me be honest about one of the main catalysts to this epic adventure: love. This is not the beautiful, soul-satisfying, I-can-die-now-because-I-had-it kinda love. I'm talking about the sloppy, discombobulated, possibly eternally unrequited love that masks itself as historical and real. This is the kind of love that has permeated my life experiences for decades, and it is one of the reasons I came on this trip to find the metaphoric scissors I need to snip those connections: past, present, and future.

Oh. You gonna ghost now and profess your affection later? *Snip*. You gonna call me crying in your drunkenness about how I'm the only one that ever truly loved you, meanwhile never committing yourself to me? *Snip*. You gonna hold me all through the night like we were always meant to be together, then get another girl's number right in front of me the next day? (You think I didn't notice?) *Snip*.

You get the point.

I could hear the swishing slices of the scissors as I drifted off into sleep.

Space

Sometimes empty moments
Are torture to the soul,
Full of self-doubt,
Conspiracy theories
And irrational bouts of panic.

Sometimes the sinister silence
Brings agonizing frenzies
Of self-reflections,
Regret,
And a sense of rejection.

Sometimes the ravenous space
Craves acknowledgment,
Affirmation, confirmation.
The waiting turns
To a preoccupation
Of undignified desperation.

But this time,
My soul seeks solace
In the quiet still
Of nothingness.
Thoughts cease.
Scrutiny comes to a halt,
And I breathe.

Process.

The space makes room
For clarity.

Surely it will come.

No Games Required

When I wake up in the morning, I can see that the only clarity I have in terms of my failed relationships begins with my own self-awareness.

The pressure of exuding feminine perfection in order to get the man you want is utterly overwhelming to me. If not screwing up is a prerequisite for real love, then sign me up for the convent; I would rather be a nun. Despite my intellect and education level, I'm a fool in matters of the heart. I am untamed and impatient, and I give myself to hope and opportunity with reckless abandon. With that inevitably comes myriad mistakes and, often, even regrets.

Steve Harvey would throw me out with the bath water.

I know I don't play a good game. I don't even know the positions. It's just me, standing on the football field, wondering what quarter we are in. My equipment is love, passion, optimism, loyalty, dedication…and a smorgasbord of imperfections.

I will not make the perfect first or second impression. I will not wait proper wait times. I'll text too much and share too much. I'll probably make it weird at times with the ramblings of my brain. I will withdraw awkwardly if I feel too vulnerable or detect a hint of rejection. I'll over-analyze the relationship at all hours of the night, and if I'm not brave enough, I'll run so fast from you that you won't even know why. And if I'm brave, I'll give myself to the moment and what feels right, and I'll pray it wasn't wrong and that you don't judge me for it.

My hands carry the world in them. They are independent, strong, and capable. They are providers to so many hearts. Sometimes, I'm so busy juggling the hearts of others in those hands that perhaps there's just no room for my own.

So this heart of mine fumbles around and makes its own decisions, some spontaneous and others premeditated. It is courageous and fearful, bold and battered.

It may not be the perfect process, but the man that finally sees this heart will treasure it and accept me just the way I am, flaws and all. The one whose heart is for me will love this imperfect presentation and understand the truth and beauty of my true self.

No games required.

Chapter Two
Day 2: Thoughts by the Ocean

I had realized that the old doors of my hotel may be the loudest closing doors ever made, and the people near me apparently have a passion for incessantly slamming them. This startling phenomenon started this morning at 6 a.m., despite the hotel's no noise from midnight until 8am policy. The neighbors also liked to cackle and talk loudly in the hallway during that time frame as well. Shoot me.

However, breakfast arrived at 9:15 a.m. as requested, and it was every bit as hot, savory, and fresh as last night's meal. The three-egg omelet with toast actually came with potatoes, too, and was enough food for three people. I forced my-

self to eat half the eggs and toast (no potatoes), only because I was trying to get my money's worth. I am a true coffee snob, and they did not disappoint. It may actually have been the best coffee I ever had, so silky and nutty that I stayed in bed an extra hour just to savor every sip and to recover from the early morning assaults from my neighbors.

Finally, I made my way to Rockport. I found a tiny, secluded beach called Pebble Beach.

Pebble Beach

Pebble Beach is tranquil and apparently a well-kept secret. The waves are calm and soothing to the soul, and you can come with nothing but two complimentary waters from the hotel and whatever else you can fit into a small backpack. I perched myself on a large, hot rock with no one within 60 yards of me. Parking is free, as there is no one here but God and the ocean.

I wanted to see if I could sit on the rocky cliffs before I left this beach.

The longer I stared at the smooth, vacillating waves, random thoughts invaded my mind.

1.   I'm wondering if my best friend is secretly watching me on Find my Friends since I didn't tell her where I was going on this trip. I just told her I was going to disappear for a week and

to not freak out. I'm also hoping she is okay because she has been going through a house crisis this summer, and it hasn't been easy. I'm hoping my disappearing to take this trip hasn't caused her any annoyance or resentment while she is back home dealing with all of life's troubles.

2. I'm hoping I see a whale while I'm sitting here.

3. I'm also hoping some rich man finds me today and invites me on his yacht to drink expensive wine and go deeper into the ocean, where the waves are turbulent and dangerous, where the sea better reflects my insides. I don't even care if he is 100 years old.

4. My kids are my life. Being home without them for a week would be like being home without my soul, which was another main factor in this escape. I only brought two pieces of jewelry on this trip, and both are linked to my children. One is a silver necklace with a family tree and a quote about family that Jaden, my oldest, picked out for me one year at Christmas. The other has two dog tags on a chain, and each tag has a piece of artwork on it. One was made by Miles, my youngest, and the other by Jaden. My children are literally and figuratively on my heart every day.

5. The air in New England is salty and fishy.

6. I'm getting hungry and have nothing but water with me on this trip. Maybe I'll lose weight? Not if I keep eating out though.

7. Seaweed here is extravagant. There is a sienna red variety that looks like a chunk of hair that has been ripped out. There is another kind that looks like dried up kale, and it comes in gold and eggplant colors. There's also a green stalk with bean-like things on it that resembles some type of seaweed edamame. I'm wondering why New England gets all the good seaweed.

8.   The water here is straight-up melted ice cubes. It is nothing like the warm, southern, coastal beaches. Only crazy white people would enter these arctic waters. You know, the ones that wear shorts outside in a blizzard.

Okay, after leaving the beach to explore the quaint little town of Rockport, I decided it was a bust. All it did was make me miss my kids and wish I were skinny. There is absolutely no reason why this town made me wish I were skinny, other than it's a place my mind often goes to without any rhyme or reason.

Fighting my girthy thighs and floppy arms and belly is apparently my favorite pastime. I've been doing it since as far back as I have memory, literally. I've been on one diet or another since as long as I can remember being alive. Sadly, as soon as I could write, I began lamenting in my first ever journal about how I was mad at my mother for being concerned about my weight and only letting me have a half a bowl of cereal when I wanted a full bowl.

I vented my frustrations about my weight and mother for years in that little white diary with pastel flowers decorating the cover, and I still remember the day she found it and read it. I don't remember ever talking about it; but just knowing the fact that she had read it is enough. Now that I'm grown, I know she only had the best intentions worrying about my weight, knowing how hard the road ahead of me in airbrushed America would be if I never fit the social norm, and she was right. To this day, I wonder if I would have had less unrequited love if only I wasn't overweight. That issue in itself is one of the great trifecta I came on this trip to overcome: self-acceptance. I'm not saying I have to stay fat my entire life, but I'm ready to love myself where I'm at, not insult myself every time I look at a picture of myself or try on jeans in a dressing room. I'll always strive for better health, but I don't have to hate my reflection on the journey.

As for Rockport making me miss my kids, each quirky little shop and ice cream parlor was full of an array of knick knacks and treats, all of which I knew my kids would enjoy. To me, every glorious item stirred up the smoldering sadness of missing them that I've been running from.

Two Thumbs Up!

The best part of Rockport was leaving it. In a stubborn attempt to find a better view of the ocean, I hopped on 127 N, windows down, music blaring in the rental car, and no GPS in sight. I was several songs north when I stumbled upon a little piece of heaven called the Lobster Pool. It looks like a small red barn on the edge of the water, but I could tell by the crowded lot in the middle of the afternoon that it must be good. Naturally, I stopped. So much for my dreams of being skinny.

You can sit inside or outside at the Lobster Pool, and either way you get a direct view of the ocean. The restaurant also redeemed the lobster roll for me. This time I had the plain kind with butter on the side. Lobsters are pulled from the tank and cooked to order. Mine was firm, sweet, and melted in my mouth. The table next to me had a table full of fried sides, and I DESPERATELY wanted to dive head-first into everything on their plates. I envisioned myself motorboating my face in a basket of hush puppies. I tried to eat the healthiest options instead, which was a 140-calorie bag of Cape Cod chips. It turns out this place is BYOB, which I would have done if I had known.

This would be a great place to chill with my bestie at a table outside in the evening, drinking wine and nibbling on hot fries. This thought makes me miss her so much that I break my off-the-grid rule and text her images of my view, letting her know how much I wished she were there with me.

Front and Rear View at the Lobster Roll

Chapter Three

Day Two Continued: Drinking Tom Selleck's Mustache

After I left the Lobster Roll, I went back to Beverly, a town near Salem, and bought a car phone charger, water bottles, and a can of nuts from a local dollar store.

I showered and got dressed to go out.

I found an Irish Pub that is within walking distance from my hotel and decided that would be a great place for some early evening drinking. Upon my arrival, trivia was supposed to start in ten minutes, so I decided to just sit and wait, making awkward eye contact with a bearded white guy across the room. *Slim pickins,* I thought to myself. It would have been nice to have someone to talk to and buy me drinks! However, the bearded

stranger probably thought I was weird, considering the fact that I was now sitting in this bar, writing in a journal, and chugging alcohol.

I planned to check out karaoke at a place called OPUS at 9. I was just trying to enjoy my last night of civilization before I went to live in

(Hotel Room Selfie Before Heading to Bar)

a camper with no water, somewhere in the mountains for a few days. Maybe there I would be able to quiet the secret screams that no one knows exist but me.

Minutes later, I learned that karaoke doesn't exist at the OPUS anymore, so instead I wandered into a strange bar/coffee shop with girls posing in period piece clothing from the 1930s and '40s and men attempting to draw them while simultaneously concealing their erections. Drinking an overly-sweet, hard drink, called "Tom Selleck's Mustache," I began wondering what world I just stumbled into.

Since I was already there, sipping overpriced alcohol, I figured I might as well join in the somewhat unnerving fun. I only had a pen on hand, but I attempted to draw the '40s era model in my journal, as if that were my plan all along. Considering I was unable to erase anything and that it only took me about three minutes to complete it, my drawing really wasn't half bad. I showed it to the model af-  terwards, and she took a picture and decided to use it as her Facebook profile pic. I guess that makes me some kind of famous.

I ended up hanging out with the model and two of her friends. We all crammed onto a squishy brown leather couch, and we played an '80s and '90s trivia card game. We connected, laughed, and talked into the early morning hours. I never asked their ages, but I could tell they were one or two decades younger than me and had no idea how old I was, which did not matter. They were very decent people, and we were just humans having fun.

The youngest gave me a smoke after, and we talked about life goals and other typical tipsy topics. I found out he was only 21 and had a night job delivering papers, but his real dream was to go to art school. He told me he sleeps in the parking lot. It took a minute for me to register what he was saying. It is so sad that someone so young could have a job and still be homeless. I asked about his parents, and he got quiet.

At that time, the two others came out to join us, and I saw him sneak off really quickly, presumably ashamed of the confession he had made to a complete stranger. He was gone, and I did not even know his name. None of us exchanged names, actually. I thought about introducing myself to them a few times that night, but it seemed strangely inappropriate as we had already bonded somehow on a deeper level.

These two semi-drunk strangers walked me back to my hotel, and they wished me well on my next adventure with hugs and a silent church-money-to-palm maneuver, except they slipped me mace instead of money. They were worried about me trekking alone and insisted I take it for protection.

Even as we walked the dark streets back to my hotel, I was overwhelmed by the openness and acceptance of these strangers. So many people go through life guarded and judgmental; I've never really been one of those people, and it often leads me to see humanity in a different light than many of my friends. On one hand, it puts me at risk for getting hurt more often, but it also keeps me stumbling into kindness, generosity, and inspiration through random connection. It is a gift God has always given me. My ex-husband used to joke that I never knew a stranger. I could meet someone in line at the grocery store and have them over for dinner the next night.

Perhaps the greatest example of my openness and willingness to accept strangers is how I met my long-time friend, Leslie. Before children and early on in my marriage, I made a habit of going to the gym at 5 am every morning. That gave me two hours to work out and one hour to shower, get dressed, and drive to work by 8 a.m. Being a night owl, I would often pack my bag the night before and sleep in my workout clothes in order not to be tempted to stay in bed the next morning.

Something must have gone wrong in my packing the night before because I had forgotten to pack an essential element: a bra. Now, after a two-hour workout, my clothes, including sports bra, would be drenched. There was no way I'd be putting on a wet sports bra under my professional work attire. I was an operations manager at a brokerage firm at the time, and I always dressed to the nines.

My ex-husband was working the night shift as a custodian, so when I realized my mistake, I started blowing up his phone to no avail; the man could sleep through an earthquake. So I put on my black pantyhose and knee-length black skirt, topped off with a form-fitted, bubble gum pink, slinky top.

Afraid to look in the mirror, I began talking to the only other person in the dressing room. It was a woman that I had seen regularly working out at the same time as me, but we had never spoken. I told her of my mistake and asked her to look at my chest and give me an honest evaluation.

"It's not that bad," she sweetly replied. Relieved at the good news, I confidently marched up to the mirror and nearly jumped at the vision.

"Not that bad!" I hollered. "I look like a French prostitute!" You couldn't just see my still perky (I was still in my twenties, y'all) breasts and erect nipples, you could even see the outlines of my areolas.

"I was trying to be nice," she admitted, looking sheepish now.

In an act of desperation to beat the clock and make it to work in the next five minutes, I threw on my raggedy, torn, light gray hoodie over my elegant, pink top. Minutes later, I walked into work, head high, refusing to acknowledge that there was anything awry with my completely bizarre outfit. Luckily, everyone respected me enough not to comment to my face, but I'm sure there were a few laughs behind my back.

The next morning, I was once again getting dressed before work in the gym locker room when the same lady from the day before looked at me with a panicked face. "You're not going to believe this, but I forgot my bra!"

"Don't worry, I packed two!" I shouted with a giant smile as I whipped out two bras, one in each hand, one black and one cream. "I was so worried that I was going to make the same mistake that I packed two!"

She immediately accepted my gift, learning that we both happened to wear the same size. Hurriedly she dressed, and she turned around right before she walked out of the door and said, "By the way, my name is Leslie."

"I'm Laura," I laughed, and then she was gone.

The next morning, I was hitting the exercise bike on my own, no Leslie in sight. Right before I was done, she showed up with my bra freshly laundered and stashed in a plastic grocery bag.

"Here's your bra. I washed it, and my husband wanted to know if I was wearing your panties, too!" She said rather loudly. We both burst into cackles, and that was the beginning of one of the truest, most rewarding friendships I've ever known, now nearly 20 years in the making.

Currently walking the streets of Salem with two new, nameless friends, I was almost in tears of gratitude as I soaked in yet another divine moment. This couple was tangible evidence of the good outweighing the bad in this world, of kindness and connection winning over selfishness and aloneness. I wished I had more than mere words to thank this couple (but decided to hold on to my bra) as they went out of their way to protect me on this walk home and on my journey ahead.

Chapter Four
Night-time Reflections

Once back in the safety of my own room, my heart and mind still bursting with joy and gratitude from the couple walking me home, I began to reflect on the hideous and hilarious dates I've had after my divorce. Mind you, the last time I dated was before cell phones were prominent, so I was WAAAAAAY out of the loop.

The first guy that asked me out after my separation was someone I met at my neighbor's house. Apparently, he asked for my number, which they gave, and he texted me and asked me out. Beyond offended by this modern approach, I walked next door and told my friends that if this man wanted to ask me out, then he needed to ask me to my face. Clearly, I didn't know how things worked yet.

Sure enough, just an hour or so later, the man was at my front door asking me on a date. I said yes, but I honestly wasn't ready yet and never actually went.

Eventually, I was ready to brave the dating waters, but this dip in the ocean was brief. They say there are plenty of fish in the sea, but no one ever promised they were worth catching. Here are four of the top reasons why I bolted out of the water and exchanged my swimsuit for a parka.

1. The Nose Rapist

This guy started off strong. He was a bank executive, a divorced single parent, and loved Jesus and running. Conversation was easy, fun, and intellectual, and we had an equally-yoked passion for wine. He would cook for me the most delicious of foods, and we even became running partners, frequenting the trails at Metroparks around the city.

Things took a sour turn one romantic evening on the couch. We were a good bottle of wine in when he kissed me. Mind you, this was the first kiss since my divorce, the first kiss in 13 years that didn't come from my husband. About 30 seconds in, his mouth headed north and landed on my nose. Slobber mixed with snot in what appeared to be passionate intention.

This has to be a mistake, I thought to myself. *He must be drunk and not realize what he is doing.* With this in mind, I jutted my head back, raising my puckered lips up to his lips and tongue.

To my shock, he readjusted northbound to relatch on my nasal tip. At this point, I froze. Panic. Questions darted through my mind as he rotated his tongue in and out of each nostril. *How much has changed in the dating world since I've been gone? Is this what people are doing now?!*

After the shock of my nasal cavity being violated wore off, I made an excuse to end the evening. Minutes later, I was ushering this now strange creature of a man out of my front door. I darted to my phone the instant I forced the clicking of the door lock.

Google: French kissing nose
Search results: no results found

Google: nose kissing

Search results: no results found

Wait. If Google can't even make sense out of what just happened, then surely this is not a normal thing. Relief and disgust took their turns rushing over me. Relief that the world isn't as different than it was the last time I dated. Disgust then trying to process what in the world this man was into. What kind of fetish is this? All I knew at this point was that I had no intention of finding out. This man was out.

A few years later, I was reminded of this nose kisser when I was standing in the checkout line at Sam's Club with my youngest son. An older man behind us kept making small talk with me, something about being upset they no longer carried his brand of yogurt.

As I was waiting for my receipt, the man said, "You are beautiful. I like your nose."

Crickets. My body tensed, and my face began to crinkle in confusion.

"Miles. Did you hear what that man just said to me?" I leaned down and whispered in his ear. "How bizarre!"

"I know, mom! I HATE your nose!" he passionately replied without any attempt to keep our conversation private. I grabbed his hand in one of my hands and the cart in my other, and we hightailed it out of there. We loaded the groceries into the trunk, laughing. We hopped in the car, and I promptly posted on Facebook about how odd my life is.

2. The Spirit of Jezebel Man

Where do I start with this one? He was an elementary school principal, divorced with children, and apparently had a significant amount of baby-mama drama. Dating him was like dating the Apostle Paul, or another passionate follower of Jesus.

My phone would ding throughout the day with various scriptures to encourage and inspire me. I was working at a Christian high school at the time, so I was kinda feeling his religious heart. I even looked forward to our evening chats, when he would often share a scripture and we'd get into a lengthy conversation relating it to our lives.

Wow. God actually gave me a good one this time!

Weeks went on with this type of innocent relationship, and, at first, the dates were just as fun and easy as the late night chats. One day we were exploring Barnes and Noble, feeding my book addition, and he paused, looked me up and down, and said, "I'm not usually into thick girls, but you do something to me that I can't explain."

What kind of veiled compliment was that? He had no idea that he was setting off my shame trigger of weight insecurity, so I cut him some slack. I guess he meant it as a compliment? (My eyebrows are twisted up so hard, even now as I recall this comment.)

Weeks later, on Valentine's Day, we were dining at a popular restaurant at Easton Mall, and the place was packed solid. Earlier, he had picked me up for the date and was all worked up about something called the "Spirit of Jezebel." Passionately ranting about his mother, his ex-wife, and his boss, all supposedly in bondage to the Spirit of Jezebel. He went on the entire drive to the restaurant; he left me speechless. This was certainly not typical Valentine's Day banter.

Once inside the restaurant, the rant continued. All the while, I kept thinking, *Geez. His mom has it. His boss has it. His ex-wife has it...Does he think I have it, too?* I was too afraid to ask.

I did, however, dare to ask him to explain exactly what the spirit was. I'm not really sure what he said because halfway through the explanation he began speaking in tongues, at the TOP OF HIS LUNGS. You could literally hear forks dropping as what felt like billions of heads turned to see the bizarre scene going down at our table.

If anyone has been to a spirit-filled church, you may know of the term speaking in tongues, but if you haven't, it is hard to describe. Suffice it to say, he was shouting out lengthy strands of words that don't belong to any human language, with drastic emphasis accenting certain words.

My face began to burn with all the heat in the deepest layer of hell. What do I do now? I contemplated slowly sliding down out of my chair and slithering out like a snake on the floor. Maybe his religious gibberish would deter their eyes from my own bizarre escape.

But no, I sat there, frozen. Approximately 10 years later, he was covered in sweat and sat back down and finished his meal. I didn't dare say another word.

The silence on the drive back was broken with his voice, now returned to its normal decimal and the English language. "So. I know we've been dating for a while now, but I have to admit that I'm not ready for a serious relationship. Can we just be friends with benefits?"

Are you SERIOUS?! What kind of hypocritical foolery was this? "Of course not!" the words oozed out with every bit of confused, religious judgment as possible. "Really? You just prayed in tongues loud enough for the entire City of Columbus to hear you, ranting about some spirit, and you have the nerve to ask me this?!"

We pulled up to my house. I slammed his car door shut for emphasis, marched my English-praying butt up my front steps, and in a swooping, overly intentional arm gesture, I slammed the door shut on his face forever.

3. The Phallic Gesturer

He was an architect, divorced with twin kids, and he was actually a two-date wonder. Date number one was utterly fabulous. We had a delicious dinner out, followed by Latin dancing into the early morning hours of the night. Truly, we had a blast.

Date two occurred at a fancy Italian restaurant, with warm lighting, red wine, and romance seeping from the walls. Our bottle of wine was delivered to the table, and right after the first sip, he asked, "So. Tonight are you going to…", and he completed the sentence with an utterly childish and vulgar phallic gesture. It's the one where you jut your tongue into your cheek while simultaneously jerking your fist in the same direction with the thumb out, representing an erect penis.

My eyes began to bulge, and my jaw dropped. Such a gesture was a complete 180 turn from the perfect gentleman that he was on our first date. I was taken aback.

Immediately backpedaling, he laughed and claimed he was just joking. Now, I'm no fool. A grown, professional male doesn't joke like that unless he's trying to gauge the situation. I gave him a stern look of "Watch yourself," and kept drinking.

Not 15 minutes later, he did it again. "So, really. Tonight are you going to...", complete with the phallic gesture.

This time I didn't hide my anger. "Look. That is not a joke. Why do you keep saying that? It's rude, and I don't like it."

"I'm sorry. I'm sorry. Honestly, I'm just joking," he giggled.

With lowered brows and pursed lips, I just glared, debating if I was going to walk out. *One last chance,* I told myself.

Now, you know where this story is heading. Of course he did it again. And this time, I was enraged. I stood straight up from my seat, knocking it off balance with my speed.

"Look! I don't know who you think you are, but you need to TAKE YOUR *** TO MAIN STREET!" I yelled while dramatically pointing in the air through the crowded room in the direction of Main Street, "because I AM NOT THAT TYPE OF WOMAN!"

With that I grabbed my purse, head high despite just making a scene in a nice restaurant, and marched towards the door. Sadly, dude chased after me, and I can still remember the exact spot I was standing in the entryway when he got up to me, for it was this moment that he thought it was appropriate to lift up the back of my skirt, grab my butt, and expose my black lace undies to God knows who.

I spun around and decked him and took off running to my car. Once safely in my Sonata, I called my friend, Nick, the same one that I always gave my location to before a date. The same friend that texts me during my dates to make sure I'm okay. The same friend I never thought I'd have to call with a real situation like this. That night I drove to his house instead, not wanting to risk possibly being followed.

(*Stop*. Before your mind rushes again and attempts to turn my life into a generic romantic-comedy, I have to tell you, Nick is gay, so don't even think it.)

In that moment, even with taking safety precautions and being in a public space, I knew that I had just escaped a possibly much worse situation. The world can be dark and scary, and I thanked God for his protection. From this point on I vowed to reserve judgment on a man's character much later in the game, after he's had more time to reveal his true motives. No longer would I be fooled by first date perfection.

4. The Naked Pooper

This one had a fancy job in the tech world, was former Navy, and had a really fun personality. Now, to be our age and never previously married maybe should have been a red flag, but he seemed so sweet and normal that I was willing to see what he was about.

Our first date was on a Sunday night at a local cantina. We both parked in the garage at the same time and found each other. Now, at first glance, I was somewhat surprised to see the extent of the wrinkles of his light pink Oxford button up shirt. It looked strangely reminiscent to the wads of balled up paper I find on my classroom floor at the end of the day. He had mentioned that he had been resting in bed most of the day, so I figured he just rolled out of bed to meet me. No harm, no foul.

"Thanks for meeting me, even though you mentioned resting a bit today. Did you come straight from bed?" I asked in the sweetest tone, trying to mask the motive behind my question.

"Oh no! I got up and got changed, so I could meet you."

Okay...

"Aww. Thanks! I'm so glad we can finally meet up in person," I admitted sincerely.

On the walk in, he began rubbing his belly, stating that it had been upset all day. I suggested maybe we skip dinner then and just have a drink, but he insisted a drink would be even worse for his stomach issues.

Okay...

The meal was a smash hit. Conversation was fun, flirty, and light—a perfect first date trifecta. After the meal, we went for a walk around the nearby creek. Suddenly, a silly yet panicked look took over his face.

"Hey, I'm really loving spending time with you and don't want this date to end, but I just have to run home real quickly and am going to come right back," he stated, as if perfectly normal.

"No worries. I had fun, too. Let's just call it a night and meet up another time."

"No! I don't want the date to be over," he protested. "I just need to run home, which is about 15 minutes away, and then I'll be right back. I don't want the date to be over."

Okay...

"Seriously, let's just call it a night. Go do whatever it is you have to do, and we can catch up another time."

His face then transformed into a stern, knowing smile, and he said, "You know what it is I have to do at home, don't you?"

"No," I lied.

"I have to take a shit."

"You know, there was a bathroom in the restaurant, and there is actually another one right here." I pointed to the public restroom just yards away from us.

"I know, but I don't shit in public."

Okay...

Now this isn't the first time I've heard a guy say this, but the situation was just so out of place. I had just met him, and I took pause at his transparency. I also thought, *How serious is your aversion to pooping in public that you literally want to leave your first date waiting by a creek at night for God knows how long while you run home to defecate? And what kind of woman would be okay with this?*

"Seriously, just go home and handle your business. It's all good."

This is when he should have bowed out of the date gracefully, but I had no such luck. Instead, he began to deliver a doctoral dissertation on his process for using the restroom and why he can't do it in public.

"I have to take my shirt off when I sit on the pot. I need to let all the muscles relax in order to get it all out," he said while simultaneously rubbing down his abdomen muscles as if giving me a reenactment of defecation. From this point on, I stood there, frozen, listening to his detailed shit speech, but all I honestly could hear was the Charlie Brown teacher voice: *wah wah, wah wah.*

Look. Anyone that knows me knows I can't handle bodily functions. I gagged changing my own kids' diapers, for crying out loud. The last thing I needed was a visual of this stranger and his bowel movements.

Somehow I managed to graciously end the date while trying to salvage his dignity. He just opened up to me on quite a personal level, and I didn't want to shame him, but I NEEDED IT TO STOP.

"I'm going to leave now," I said. "I had a great time with you as well but need to get home now to prepare for work tomorrow." I got in my car to go home, pedal to the metal, and my phone rang. It was him.

"Hello?" I asked with hesitation.

"Hi. I'm so sorry. I feel like maybe I just ruined things by telling you I take my shirt off when I shit. Is there any way I can make it up to you?"

"You're good. I don't mind. Just go home and take care of yourself," I said with sincerity now.

He probably pooped himself on the way home.

That was the last time either one of us ever tried to contact the other.

* *

Shutting my eyes to sleep for the night, I decided I probably needed the stranger's mace more for my dating life than whatever was to come before me in the mountains.

Chapter Five
Day Three, Brattleboro

- Woke up with a headache, to no surprise.

- Checked out of the hotel at 11 a.m.

- Bought Danish at an artisan bakery.

- Drove to Brattleboro, Vermont.

- Met the two NICEST people on the planet, named Bill and Becky.

Bill is a pastor, and Becky is a nurse and educator. He looks just like my friend, Matt, probably because Matt is his nephew.

One day I was drinking outside at a picnic table with Matt and his wife, Rose, and I randomly asked if they knew anyone in Vermont because I felt like going on a trip. To my surprise, Matt mentioned his aunt and uncle and ultimately connected us on Facebook.

Just moments after meeting me, Bill gave me a tour of their home, of the camper I would be staying in, and then of downtown Brattleboro. He and Becky had more work to do before their day was up, so I explored the town for a couple hours by myself as they finished up.

Brattleboro, Vermont, is the place to explore if you are looking to rack up flights of steps on your Fitbit. The town is gloriously located in the foothills of the Green Mountains. The buildings all appear to be over 200 years old and full of charm and character. The town has an artsy vibe and is full of unique stores.

At Bill's recommendation, I got a cup of iced coffee from Mocha Joe's coffee shop. The cafe is in the basement of an old brick building, and I felt that I climbed down the steps into a secret, underground cool-person cafe. I wanted to stay and relax in the ambiance, but I was too eager to get back outside.

I got sucked into a unique bookstore called "Mysteries on Main," which happens to be my favorite genre. I talked the dude's ear off in there, much to his apparent chagrin, then I bought a book, of course, and moved along.

(My home in Vermont for Two Days)

Back on the sidewalk, some shirtless, sun-bronzed man with at least a dozen 4-inch scars on his chest asked me for seven cents. Yes. Seven cents. I asked why, and he said that was all he needed to get an ice cold drink. Convinced he was legit, I gave him a quarter.

Not even a minute later, I bumped into him again, talking to a man clearly selling him drugs and telling him he just needed one more dollar. We made awkward eye contact, and he smiled, knowing I understood the transaction going down. Why did he ask for seven cents if he needed a dollar? It was strange, but I trucked out of there, looking back a couple times to see if he was watching me, which he was.

After work, Bill and Becky treated me to a nice restaurant for dinner. Happily, I devoured a unique cheeseburger that was slathered in peanut butter, eager to eat something that I couldn't find at a restaurant back home. It was just okay. Nothing special, actually. I tried to pay as a thank you for allowing me to crash on their property, but they both refused. These were total strangers, taking me in and treating me like a valued guest. I had to hold back tears at their selfless generosity and kindness.

I wondered if they had doubts at any point in time, praying I didn't turn out to be some criminal avoiding capture or a drug addicted prostitute hiding from a pimp. Or maybe God just gave them a peace about letting a total stranger stay with them, and they could take me in without fear. They never said.

After dinner, I set out on my first Vermont trail. It was raining slightly, but I would not be deterred. The Earth beckoned me.

It was a trap.

It took about 30 minutes, and I was lost, being attacked at length by apocalyptic swarms of mosquitoes. Fleeing from the mini demons devouring my flesh, I soon went off the trail and ended up climbing upward atop a small cliff. I landed in someone's backyard. Shamelessly, I walked through their neighborhood like a night stalker, covered in mud. Eventually, I found a main road and strutted my dirty butt back to the trail and into my car.

This first bite of Vermont's wild nature, which I so desperately had craved, should have been a giant red flag. This should have been the moment that I began rethinking my impending adventure. Alas, it was not.

That night, back at the waterless trailer that I was borrowing on those kind strangers' property, I delved into a variety of pamphlets and books about the Appalachian Trail, searching for the perfect journey. After an hour or so, it was decided. Some dude back in the '70s wrote a book and stated that there was a perfect little 12-mile hike on The Appalachian Trail that was ever so easy—perfect for a day trip, and he said exactly where to enter that portion of the trail. He literally said all you would need for it was a fanny pack. Yes. A freaking fanny pack.

I was ecstatic! This was a perfect trail for me. A chronic exerciser from birth, I scoffed at the challenge. I figured I could do about four miles per hour, so this breezy excursion should take about three hours. Simple! I added an extra hour into my calculation, so I could sit on top of a mountain somewhere and journal about what a victorious life I am living. Four hours tops. Done.

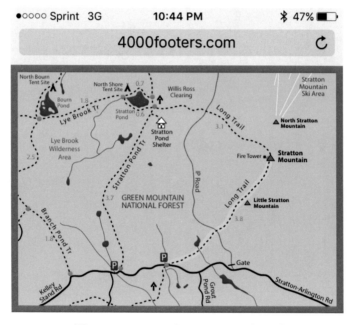

(This picture was my only companion on the trail)

Part 2
The Appalachian Trail

APPALACHIAN/LONG TRAIL

KELLEY STAND ROAD TRAILHEAD

Chapter Six
Day 4—Part 1, Uphill

9 a.m. Chatted with Becky and her granddaughter, Willow, over coffee and ate one, singular piece of toast. It was a delightful chat. I checked the weather and saw there was nothing but blue skies ahead, so I took my time getting to the trail.

10 a.m. Ate a bunch of samples at a cheese factory that I passed on the way to the trail.

10:20 a.m. Drove an hour to the part of the Appalachian Trail (Green Mountains) called Stratton Loop. Like I said, it was a 12-mile trail with a 4,000-foot mountain to conquer.

11:30 a.m. Parked my car on the base of a mountain and started the trail with nothing but a toddler backpack containing the following items:

- One roll of toilet paper
- Bug spray
- Oat crackers
- 4 plastic bottles of water from the dollar store
- Beef jerky
- My phone, ID, and rental car key
- My journal and a pen
- Mace from a stranger

Oh, did I mention I was wearing regular old tennis shoes as well? Yep. A straight up city girl deep in the wilderness with nothing but high hopes, smiles, and the good Lord above.

(Scan the QR code with an iPhone camera or QR code reader app to view the video.)

I thought there would be a build up to the mountain. I didn't realize that you immediately start on an incline, climbing a "smaller" mountain on the way to Big Bertha. I was exhausted and huffing and puffing within 10 minutes, which I thought was hysterical. I whipped out my phone and decided to capture the moment in a video for my bestie and her kids (my godchildren).

What the dude didn't consider in his cute little book about easy Appalachian Trail day trips is the amount of woman on these bones that I'd be hoisting up those mountains. In addition, he forgot to mention that there really is no actual trail in this section. There's just the ever-faintest hint of a trodden path, almost entirely up small, flat rocks, which are jarring out of the uneven dirt scattered upon the mountain.

Now look, I wasn't expecting a paved or even manicured natural trail by any stretch of the imagination, but I did expect an occasional sign from time to time or somewhat of a sunken dirt path to guide the way. Dude should have told me to take a compass or whatever hikers use to find their way in the wilderness. But, he did not. He just said to bring a fanny pack.

The trail was rugged, narrow, rocky, and rooty, and I blame the upcoming atrocities entirely on '70s dude. Clearly, he is either a sadistic liar or the super mountain climber champion of the universe. There was absolutely NOTHING easy about this trail.

In my amazing pre-hike calculations, I didn't consider how steep and rugged and never-ending this climb would be. I'm pretty sure I scared all the wildlife off the entire mountain with all my heavy breathing and cries out to God. I was fully aware of the fact that I sounded like an adult film star the entire 2 ½ hours it took me to reach the top of the first mountain. I had no choice, nor did I care.

My verbal explosions were the only somewhat sense of relief that I had against the cruelty of the mountain. Many times, I felt as though I was a participant getting sick on some ridiculously over-the-top challenge on the old show, *The Biggest Loser*.

I wondered what had so confidently inspired this chunky, almost 40-year-old woman, with an anus full of hemorrhoids (don't ask) to embark on this obvious act of stupidity. Clearly, I now understand that I needed to train for this, like the strange people that have always annoyed me on what appeared to be their ostentatious show of superior physique as they climb pretend mountains on that massive, showy machine at the gym. God, how I wished I had practiced on that stupid machine. But here I am, knee deep in my life choices, too stubborn to turn back.

Now, as my tiny backpack feels like a pregnant elephant dangling from my shoulders, I see it is this over-optimistic, I-can-do-anything attitude that has once again put me in a nearly impenetrable predicament.

While we are on the topic, let's address the toddler backpack on my shoulders. This trip was the first time I had been on a plane in over a decade. My previous travels were all pre-9/11, and I had no idea what I could pack and bring as a carry on. In my fear that a regular backpack would be too big for a carry on, I dug out a dusty old toddler backpack from my kids' closet, hoping it would pass the size test.

Imagine me now, forging ahead in the great abyss of geological and wild-life unknowns, adorned in black yoga pants, electric blue tennis shoes, a green v-neck cotton shirt, and a snazzy toddler backpack. Mount Stratton Master Climbers, meet Sore Thumb.

As I heave my way up, I can hear the *Biggest Loser* coaches giving their motivational pep talks, screaming to the loser about to quit, and in the end there are tears of joy as the fat person realizes she really can do whatever she puts her mind to do. "Just believe in yourself." It's the life lesson at the end of every winding road and the theme of every motivational speaker, and suddenly, I realize that it is crap. Total crap.

As I lug my body one rocky, sweaty, pornographic step forward, it all becomes clear: this message about life is utterly misleading. So many of us want instant gratification without the work that is needed to succeed. Even the show, *The Biggest Loser*, pushed an unhealthy, almost instanta-neous weight-loss in order to celebrate the golden calf of success: accom-plishment. We rack up accomplishments like they are the measure of our worth, and we will do whatever it takes to get them quickly.

It's not that I disagree with the truth that you can accomplish anything that you put your mind to, but sometimes there's a process you need to work through before you tackle the thing your mind has chosen. Many times have I victoriously conquered the seemingly impossible in my life, but now, on this glorious mountain, I see that racking up a resume of mere accomplishments is not the answer to life's happiness.

In fact, some of my greatest life moments have occurred when I wasn't able to accomplish my goals. The best example of this is the summer that I was suckered into being on our neighborhood dive team.

Since the age of eight, I was an eager participant, and quite successful member, of the Loch Alpine Community Swim Team and also a member of the Synchronized Swimming Team. I basically lived at the pool during the summers, from the time I woke up until it was time to ride my bike home for dinner.

Because I was always there, I was an easy target for recruitment when the diving team was short a diver to compete one season. I was hesitant, but being a chronic people-pleaser, I conceded. Now, to say I was utterly terrified of the required dives is maybe an understatement, and I believe this fear handicapped my ability to conquer them.

The front and back dives were my safety zones, and I wished that would have been the end of it, but there were four more required dives in order to compete: the double, the one and a half twist, the inward, and the reverse. Now let me tell you, I am no quitter, even when fear is involved, and I always have been a woman of my word, so I tackled those treacherous dives with all the confidence I could muster.

Over and over again I failed, enduring epic smacks upon the water that left my skin aflame. My coaches must have felt bad for me, and in their mercy, they provided me with something we called "the smack suit." The intention was that I could keep learning without my poor skin taking a beating every time my flailing body smacked upon the water. Really, all it accomplished was making me look like a scuba diver gone mad, seizing in eye-catching gyrations through the air.

The inward and reverse dives became my archenemies because messing up those dives was even worse than smacking the water; I could crack my head open on the board, break my neck, and maybe even die. It didn't help that often at the meets someone would, in fact, accidently dive into the board and injure themselves while attempting these dives.

As the season progressed, my skills did not. Nevertheless, I pushed myself up onto the board at every meet, praying to God I could accomplish something that at least resembled the required dives. I was quiet in between dives, too embarrassed to speak, but I never gave up. This was particularly hard for me as I was used to being somewhat decent at most things I attempted, both academically and athletically. It was humbling and frustrating to not be able to master the dives.

The season always ended with a district championship meet. Being that our team had only enough divers to compete, I was not off the hook. This was it, my one last shot to make the dives, for God knows I would never do this again. Ever.

As expected, I performed mediocre front and back dives. I smacked on the double, inward, and reverse, but it was my last dive, the one and a half twist, that sealed my fate. For this dive, you are supposed to do one and a half somersaults in the air while simultaneously twisting your body to a specific degree. My brain and body never computed the way in which to do this, and this day was no different.

I can still see the shape of the pool, the quiet crowd intensely staring at me, most likely praying for me too at this point, as I climbed the metal steps onto the board. With a deep breath and head held high, I gracefully stepped to the edge of the board, jumping on the end once, twice, and with a swish of my arms lifting my body up on the third jump, I catapulted high into the air.

Now, I could feel that my legs at this point were frozen in a frog-like position, knees bent outward, feet flat as if I was ready to jump, but my mind was too focused on maneuvering the top half of my body for me to correct the lower half. "Bend, flip, and twist," I told myself, but my body had other plans.

With an awkward bend and twist, I merely sailed through the air like a glorious frog, crashing with the splash of the century. The judges were soaked when they held up my scores, a unanimous "0" across the board.

I took my time coming up from under the water, deciding how I felt about the ordeal, and I began to laugh. With a giant smile, I emerged in mermaid fashion from the water as if I had just won championships. I looked at my scores as I climbed up the pool stepladder, and I said, "Well. Someone had to get last," as I chuckled all the way back to my towel.

The thing is, my smile was sincere. With the last crash into the pool, my season was over, and I was beside myself with relief, even if I failed the dive. I remember surprising myself with how much joy I found in the fact that I, a super competitive perfectionist, was not phased in any way about taking last place.

I knew that my main goal of being on the team was to help out the others, so they could compete. Of course, I wanted to do well, but I never accomplished that goal. This blatant failure was not only humbling, but it also taught me freedom to accept that it's absolutely okay to not be good at everything. I tried, kept my word, and failed, but I had never been happier with myself.

Here I am now, trying to recall exactly what goal had brought me to the Green Mountains? What was I trying to accomplish? Would my loneliness and broken heart be cured on the other side of this mountain? Of course not. Would I have a new sense of self-worth and accomplishment? Maybe, but only temporarily. Would my job miraculously pay more and all my money challenges be over? Solid no. What was I really doing out here in these mountains? What was I trying to accomplish?

Hiking the Appalachian Trail was a long-dormant goal on my Bucket List, and so I went at it with virtually zero thought. I wanted to do it, so I did. Period. There was really nothing much more to it. But this was not a Columbus Metro Park, and I was about to pay. You can't just wake up one morning and successfully hike the Appalachian Trail just because you believe in yourself. So much more was needed to succeed, but it was too late.

As I sensed the top getting closer and closer and the rocks I had been climbing getting steeper and steeper, there was a relief in my spirit. I was certain the way down would be infinitely easier. The sky began to rumble—just a slow churn of uneasiness. Slowly at first, then gradually building in speed and volume, until a friendly drizzle melded into a flat-out mountain-top monsoon. Seriously?! *Thanks, God.*

Every muscle in my body clenched as I tried not to plummet off the muddy, wet, slippery rocks, and the incline was so steep now that when I lifted a leg off the ground to brave each new step, the weight of my now nemesis of a backpack pulled me back. I teetered backwards and clenched my core with each careful step ahead while the seasoned hiking gazelles went by with a musty nod of recognition.

What I have purposely failed to mention so far is, all the freaking tall, skinny, super-hiker masters that had been breezing past me on the trail at the apparent speed of lightning. Plus, they had all these monstrous backpacks, fancy hiking boots, and what looked like ski poles, but for dirt. All the passer byers were friendly in spirit and quite rude in stench. I imagined many of these hikers were not fresh out of the shower as I was this morning.

These gazelles whooshed past me, like teachers rushing out of their classrooms on a Friday afternoon. Must be nice to not be overweight. I couldn't help but suck my teeth at them as they passed. Full judgment, like, "go ahead and eat a cake skinny, hiker guy. I'm out here climbing with bones loaded with woman, and I'm still out there living my best carb life." Despite these show-offs, I was still in good humor, even in the rain, with my foolish apparel and earth-destroying plastic, Dollar Store disposable water bottles.

Finally, I reached the top of the glorious, long-awaited, much-suffered mountain top. But wait!!! There was absolutely no majestic view of accomplishment to ingest. All that to basically stare at tree trunks. At this point, I was too tired to even lift my face upward into the passing storm to look around for anything else.

In place of a view, there was what appeared to be a chincy metal, Vermont-crafted Eiffel Tower, containing the actual stairway to heaven. This was the only way to get a view from the top of this beastly chunk of earth, and I wasn't having it. Even my thighs laughed at the thought of the additional climb. What kind of psychopaths would attempt such a brutal feat immediately after the unkind trail just travelled?

The rain began to dwindle, and I thanked God for this merciful shift in weather. I quickly sat under a tree and began my second video to my bestie. (Scan the QR code below with your iPhone camera or with a barcode reader app to see the video.) Even still, I had my wits and good attitude about me, but before I had time to finish the video or finish eating even the smallest morsel of food, the sky turned dark and angry, and so began what possibly became the worst decision of my life.

Speaking of bad life decisions, which are kinda my thing, let's recap a few others that first come to mind:

1. **Every single haircut I had in the 90's:** *Bangs ratted up in a six-inch rainbow formation around my forehead, complimented by a tight, wavy perm.*

2. **The great shoplifting spree of senior year.** *A handful of girl-friends and I had gone away for an overnight stay to a nearby town in Michigan just for fun. Prior to the exodus from our hometown, I had learned that a CD, which cost about $16 to purchase at the time, only actually cost one penny to make. I was appalled to the point that I passionately convinced my girl squad, on our drive to our weekend get-away, that corporate America owed us for overcharging us. Our revenge: shoplifting.*

   Now, we were good kids: honor roll, band nerds, religious, etc. So, we took more of a Robinhood-type approach to our robberies. Adorned in baggy clothes, we hit store after store, filling the space in our clothes with thoughtful gifts for our friends and siblings—things we knew they wanted but couldn't afford. We walked into each store at a healthy weight and walked out looking obese.

   We stashed our revenge loot in our hotel room in between runs. The only two items I can specifically recall are the following:

   1. *A Walkman my friend Laura picked up for her little brother.*

   2. *Nair. This was my first time encountering this hair removal cream, and I was amazed as my friend used it to remove her bikini hair. I thought it was quite daring at the time.*

   After a couple stores, we should have left it alone, but our "righteous" anger somewhere along the line morphed into greed, and we kept going.

It all ended with a pair of Minnie Mouse panties, the sole item I was paying for as the cashier rang me up at a Meijer's Thrifty Acres. Turns out, we had been followed for quite a while, and the security team was awaiting our escape. We were escorted back to their security room, and the cops were called.

We cried. We panicked. We tried to bargain and plea. All parents were reached by phone except mine, since they were off on vacation and this was before cell phones. Since there was one friend with us that was already 18, who didn't partake in our revenge towards corporate America, I was released to her care.

Now, in Michigan, you get tried at age 17 as an adult, and it just so happened that my friend Amy (named changed for privacy) had turned 17 the day before this all went down. So, she had to be handcuffed, taken to jail in the police car, photographed for her mug shot...the whole criminal nine yards. We all spent the evening in jail, waiting for this all to go down and talking to the arresting officer for hours. I don't remember anything else, except that they eventually let Laura go under the condition we would appear in their local court the next day for sentencing. I also remember that the police officer came to check on us at the hotel room the next morning, and we sat at a picnic table talking like old friends for hours. Now, I was too busy worrying to notice how inappropriate this was. I was afraid that he would want to see our hotel room, which would mean he could have discovered the rest of our stash of stolen goods and the illegal alcohol we had brought. That discovery would have sent us all right back to jail. Ridden with anxiety, I failed to stop to wonder why a grown man spent his morning off with a bunch of "barely legals." Looking back, I take pause at this situation.

When it came time to face the music in court, we all sat in the back of the room while the judge reamed into our friend, Amy, who just stood before her, bawling. "Whose idea was this?!" the judge screamed at our friend.

"It was my friend, Laura's!" my traitorous friend yelled back, pointing at me across the courtroom. I remember my friend, Alicia, and I busted out laughing at this inappropriate moment, probably out of embarrassment, which certainly added minutes to the tongue-lashing she continued to give our friend. I don't even remember what her punishment was; all I know is I had gotten a "Get Out of Jail Free" card, and I thanked the good Lord above.

That is until we went back home, and all of my friends had to face the music with their parents at their respective homes, and I was overridden with guilt. In an attempt to get in on the equality of the punishments, I went to each and every house and apologized to the parents for what I had done. Most of the parents forgave me, but not Amy's. Her parents were strict Catholics, and not only did they forbid her to go out the rest of the summer, but I believe they forbade her to be my friend anymore. She had been one of my best friends since seventh grade, so this was a deep wound to me. To this day, our friendship has never been repaired.

In a final act of retribution, I asked all of the parents if their children could accompany me as I confessed all the disappointing details to my own, unexpecting parents. I felt the only way to really make this right was if my parents knew as well, considering it was all my idea and all. They all agreed.

I remember knowing this was the moment my life would be over. I remember the sun shining through the wall of windows covering our living room, beaming on the cream-colored couches on which we sat. I remember being terrified to speak.

Looking back, I can only imagine what was going through my mother's mind as she sat there quietly awaiting my confession. What teenage terrors were rolling through her mental Rolodex of possibilities? AIDS? Pregnancy? Homosexuality?

"That's it?! I did so much worse than that when I was your age," she said, unimpressed, in response to my snotty-nosed, eye-watering confession and plea for forgiveness.

Crickets.

My blood-shot eyes began to bulge with utter disbelief. Was she serious? Where was my punishment? Please, mom, make me pay, so I can be set free from my sin! Now you may feel like I got off easy in this moment, but let me tell you, despite paying the penance of the 5-year ban Meijer put on us all for even entering their stores, I carry this paranoia with me to this day whenever I'm in any store. I go out of my way to make sure I'm not doing anything at all that could ever even slightly appear suspicious. I was forever changed by that bad decision.

As for the Minnie Mouse panties, I wore them like a Scarlet Letter, always reminding myself to never make that mistake again.

3. **Hairy Legs for Days.** *Just because I turned my life back towards the straight and narrow, it did not mean I lost my zeal for justice and civic outbursts. So when I learned that women shaving their legs was all a ploy from razor companies (corporate America) to make money during the war when all the men were gone and their sales dropped, I, again, was outraged.*

In my own war against injustice, I decided to stop shaving my legs. For weeks I let those bad boys grow and glisten in the sun, invoking much discussion with my socially revolting display of hair. The more people told me to shave, the longer I let it linger—to the point that I went to prom that year with my supportive, long-term boyfriend with my thick, curly hair protruding through my nylons. Months passed with this peaceful protest, and in the end, I hadn't changed the world.

4. ***The Runs—both kinds.*** *Then there was the time that I spontaneously ran a half marathon at a park without having done any training whatsoever (sounds like a recurring theme in my life). Stubborn through and through, I pushed to the end, only to find that I had given myself the worst case of the runs from the bad decision. Seriously, I had the runs for days after this, as my body tried to recover from the self-induced trauma of my innards banging around without the proper muscle structure to hold things in place. That was the last time I ever attempted a marathon, even if was only just a half.*

5. ***Dropping it like it's (not) hot.*** *More recently I was with my girls dancing at a crowded rooftop club in Vegas, and I felt the need to drop it low in my high heels and somewhat short skirt. I had made my way into a roped off VIP section of the roof to flirt and talk to the rich doctor that had rented out this section, ignoring the blatant glares of the women from his office. After clearly upsetting several of these women, I left the roped-in area to dance.*

   The Vegas skyline must have inspired the Laura of my youth, and I was in full drop when one of the girls whipped past me and knocked me over, leaving me fumbling on the ground, panties and thighs on full display through dozens of feet. Red-faced, I scurried over to my friends to tell them we had to leave, but on my way, I was stopped by a group of men. "Hey. Wasn't that you that just fell on the ground?"

   "No," I lied with disgust, then grabbed my girls and took off for the door.

And so, with a lifetime of past bad decisions egging me on, I put my phone away in my toddler backpack to protect it from the storm, and I took my first steps down Stratton Mountain.

Chapter Seven
Day 4 Continued, Downhill

It took about thirty seconds for me to learn the second life lesson on this journey. Everyone always says, "it's all downhill from here" after they finish a daunting task or particularly difficult life challenge. We say this to provide solace to the weary life traveler. It is a great metaphor taken from the literal ease of climbing back down the mountain after trying to get over the great hump.

I learned, sometimes the journey down is just as freaking difficult as climbing the beast, especially if the universe turns its back on you and decides to storm to no avail. The narrow, rocky, rooty, muddy incline I had so greatly struggled to conquer had become a literal narrow, rocky, rooty, muddy waterfall. Oh, how I wished I had those handy dirt poles to protect me on the now treacherous trail downward.

Any normal human being would have turned around and gone back to their car at this point, only being three miles into the twelve-mile trail. But, I said, "F-it," and just started high-tailing it deeper into the trail. I don't know what compels me to do these kinds of things, besides a natural-born craving in my soul for adventure for the unknown and sheer determination to do what I say I will do.

Or stupidity.

The trail was slow-going, slippery, and eternal. Apparently, the Appalachian Trail doesn't have signage along the way, and I had no clue where I was or how far I had to go.

There were a few times earlier on the trail when I had to pee so badly that I considered peeing my pants, since it was raining so viciously anyway, but the one and only dry spot on me at that time was my crotch, so I elected to drop my drawers and pee over a clump of moss, thinking it was the least likely area to poke me in places I didn't want to be poked.

Trying to pull up my sopping wet underwear and spandex yoga pants after that was extra fun, considering all the bugs that immediately swarmed my ample food source of an ass.

Several hours into the storm, my eyelashes had a steady stream of water flowing off of each eye. There was no point to try to wipe the facial stream away. There was no stopping the tempest of a storm. Likewise, my crotch had become a Niagara Falls of its own, not from urine, but from the sheer amount of water covering and pouring off of my body. I was a freaking human waterfall that was simultaneously navigating my way down a literal waterfall.

Visions of *The Biggest Loser* morphed into a solo edition of *Naked and Afraid*. I wasn't naked (yet), but I might as well have been. My clothes were plastered to my body in a way that put every curve, roll, and nipple on display.

At first, I tried to salvage my shoes in all this mess, attempting to avoid the dark mountain mud as much as possible. Straddling became my maneuver of choice, as even my short legs were long enough to straddle the slim width of the trail in many parts; however, walking in a half-squat straddle takes a toll on the thigh region, and I eventually released my last little bit of care and resigned myself to the inevitable. I just walked directly in the several-inch deep trail of water and swarthy mud.

Just when I believed the trail would never end, I hit what I knew to be the halfway point: Stratton Pond.

Now I don't know what constitutes a "pond," but this was an enormous, majestic body of water that would certainly qualify as a lake by Ohio's standards. It was breathtaking, and the rain graciously slowed to just a drizzle upon my arrival. I felt like Moses of the sky as I stood on the water's edge and the clouds turned light and separated like the Red Sea.

The expansive, calm, glorious water was surrounded by dark green evergreens and much smaller mountains. Incredible to behold. I wanted nothing but to sit and inhale its beauty, yet I had some concerns:

1. If I sat down at this point, my body would undoubtedly never move again.

2. I knew I had six more miles to go, and I was afraid that, at my pace, I'd be stuck in the mountains after dark with no supplies to survive.

Stratton Pond when the rain cleared

Against the desperate cry of my heart, I journeyed on, and not more than two minutes later, the thunder resumed its roar, and the rain began its most violent rage of all. Had God given me that tiny reprieve to encourage my soul and calm the raging tempest growing inside of me? He must have known that I needed that vision and breath to sustain me for what was coming next.

Chapter Eight
Day 4 Continued, After the Pond

In my opinion, the trails were not clearly marked, and at this point, I was unsure which path to take from the pond. I was supposed to leave the AT and switch to the Stratton Pond Trail, but no sign bore this name. In fact, there were no signs of any at the four converging paths.

Panic.

This is the point I lose all humor and begin to accept fear. My phone had not had reception for hours, so I was unable to find my location. I had taken a picture of the trail map, and once I found shelter in a trail tent beside the water, I was able to take out my phone and study the picture. It appeared that I was on the right trail, yet there was really no way to tell.

Panic rising.

I walked for about a half mile ahead and turned back to the pond to try to confirm that I was in fact on the right path. Despite walking circles around the trail intersections, I thought maybe, just maybe, I had missed a sign. I saw no one and still couldn't find a trail marked, "Stratton Pond Trail," so I turned back to the trail I had just returned from and went full force, praying to God that I was on the right trail and wasn't about to die alone in these woods.

It was about fifteen minutes later that my body began to shut down. The pain in my legs, feet, and back began to feel unbearable, but I had no choice but to move forward. It's amazing how the option of death pushes you forward in an otherwise impossible movement.

My new friend, Becky, had warned me about the bears in the mountains and told me they were easy to scare; I just had to make myself "look big." Sure. I'm 5'1½," so looking big to a bear sounded so easy and feasible. Smh.

Now, wandering in the darkness, jumping at every growl of the storm and rustle of leaves, I realized I had forgotten to ask an incredibly important question: What do I do when I make myself look big? Do I scream and make noise like a crazy person, or do I stand there quietly, looking as fierce as possible? Would my screams poke the no longer metaphorical bear?

Each rising question leads to another level of panic.

In addition, the sky was making it appear as night on the trail, and I knew in just a couple more hours, I'd be out of light entirely. I had no flashlight, almost no food, no tent, etc. My phone still had no reception and was losing battery with every passing hour.

I began to get really angry at the lack of signage on the trail. If a bear didn't kill me, I was sure the bugs would. They were on me like white on rice. Oh, how I longed for any sign of encouragement, like a distance marker. How many miles left to go? I knew this section of the trail was supposed to be about four miles, and mile markers could have helped me better determine if I was on the right path.

My body was completely done after the pond, and I honestly didn't know if I could make it to the end of wherever this trail leads. I had been on the trail for hours, and there were times that the exhaustion started to make me feel as though I was hallucinating. Every dark tree stub was a bear in my eyes, and the deep, guttural, and constant roars of the thunder easily sounded like growls.

This was the point that everything changed.

I no longer craved the solitude of wild, unadulterated nature. I just wanted to teleport home to Columbus and hug my boys.

The Metroparks of Columbus that I have so often insulted for being imperfectly, perfectly "organized nature"—so lackluster compared to the excitement of raw, uncontrolled nature that I had desired—suddenly had great value in my eyes. Back home, I know the trails. They are clear and safe, and they mark their miles. I know all their twists, turns, and landmarks well enough to mark my own miles and timeframe.

I would never judge those trails at home again. That is, if I made it home…

This life-crisis adventure tour was intended as a getaway to clear my head and, hopefully, hear God and gain some genuine, long-term peace with my life's many imperfections. But now, all I wanted was to be home and to be with the people I adore and love and who love me, too.

It turned out that I didn't need to run away to gain peace. Everywhere I went, my personal demons travelled with me. I couldn't have left those demons on the mountain top even if I wanted to. Peace was certainly not to be found on this giant mood-swing of a mountain. It had to come from somewhere else.

The things that had been bothering and depressing me, all the imperfections of my almost 40-year-old life, seemed smaller now in light of the strong desire I had to be alive and just to be with my kids, my bestie, and other loved ones again. I wanted home, and to me, home is these people. In their honor, I kept marching.

In these moments, I started to value all of the imperfections of my life—because they are mine. They make me who I am. Painful perseverance pushed me forward, back to this life I no longer wish was different. At this point, I'd have done anything to make sure I could just keep living it, imperfections and all. The storm raged on, and I stopped asking God to stop it or to give me shelter. I was just praying for strength to keep moving and for some kind of sign that I was on the right path.

None came.

My cries of pain no longer resembled an elated marital moment. The tone of my cry had become a dark and mournful moan, and my slow and steady steps became my endless Green Mile. Even the storm seemed to sing a Beethoven dirge narrating my peril.

At 30,275 steps and 263 floors climbed for the day, so far, my faithful Fitbit abandoned me, for good, murdered by a steady onslaught of water upon my body. So, all my hard work from this point on would not be recorded in my app, and this greatly bothered me—probably more than it should have.

I was still looking for a sense of accomplishment after all.

Inevitably, I slipped on one of the wet stones and tumbled several yards down the side of a mountain, rolling in the thick, black mud and bashing and ripping flesh against jagged stones. Clumps of earth smeared across my face and even into the depth of my cleavage, and I sensed I soon would be truly one with the earth. Unphased by anything at this point, I rose up like the Loch Ness Monster and journeyed on. *The Walking Dead.*

A wild abyss of famished mosquitoes ate at my flesh as the trail twisted and turned to no avail. Burning shots of pain surged through my calves, quads, hips, etc. as I pressed on. Somehow. Eventually. The path started to thin, and I cried out in relief as I saw the road emerge ahead.

Again, no signs. The storm raged harder, and after again consulting the saved photo of the map on my phone for the 100th time, I moved slow and labored up a long dirt road on the mountain side. Again, I was hoping I had turned in the right direction.

The stupid, dishonest author of that hiking book that I had consulted the night before told of the last mile being on a road, off the trail, that would ultimately take me to my car. But the road was all UP another mountain, which he conveniently left out, and it was the most excruciating walk of expiration. The Dark Angel of the Appalachian Trail was plotting my final demise.

More than once I laid flat, face down in the mud as the rain bore down upon me. I waited for death to take me. When He did not, I would crawl in slow motion, knees digging deep into the rock-ridden road, as far as I could, and then I would lay down to die again. With my face cheek-to-cheek with the mud, snot began to encrust my nostrils, but my arms were too tired to rise up to wipe it away.

Crawling. Dying. Crawling. Dying. This assassination from nature went round and round.

I started thinking of the Jews in the novel *Night,* who were literally starving, malnourished, and forced to walk 40 miles(ish) in the cold winter

snow. So many fell to their death in that cruel and inhumane circum-
stance, and I began to weep for the first time on the trip, only imagining
the pain and suffering they must have endured. Their suffering went on
for years. Mine had only been for a few hours, and I suddenly felt foolish
for my resignation.

I wondered what motivation they held on to in order to keep their limbs
moving. Mine was my boys. After every turn in the road came another,
and another, and another, and I had no way of knowing if I was even
going in the right direction. My tears joined the streams flowing down
the earth into nothingness.

At last, on one final turn in the road, my glorious white rental car came
into sight. I cried out in inexplicable relief and thanks to God, which gave
me the strength I needed to slither forward in the rain to my destination,
leaving a belly-shaped trail in the mud.

Realizing that in addition to being sopping wet, I was covered, head to
toe, inside and out, in rich, black mud. Fearing I would stain the beige
cloth seats of my rental and accrue a hefty fine, I stripped down entirely
to my flesh, placing everything else in a plastic Dollar Store bag in the
trunk.

During that naked hour of salvation, I blared the heat to try to thaw my
poor, frozen body. I drove slowly, as the rain made it nearly impossible
to see the roads. At this point, hunger kicked in, and I realized I literally
had only eaten one slice of toast and some bites of cheese (before trail)
and one oat cracker (on top of a mountain) all day, yet I had exercised 7
½ hours straight. No breaks. Not one.

Unfortunately, even a hot drink from a drive thru was out of reach as my
money was locked up in the trunk with the rest of my belongings. Being

that I was naked, I knew I couldn't stop to get it out of the trunk, so I carried on.

The rental car vents blasted waves of warm air across my raw, goose-bumped skin. Shivers convulsed through my entire body. My neck muscles clenched in tight pulls of survival as I strained to see the road through the panicked wipers in the raging rain.

A few miles from my destination, it suddenly hit me how terrifying and unbefitting it would be when I exited the car in my birthday suit, for all to see my glory. What would those kind strangers think? Surely, all their fears and hesitations of welcoming me into their home in the middle of a mid-life crisis would come true.

As being arrested for indecent exposure was not on the agenda for this trip, I knew I had to do something. So, I called the sweet family, whom I had just met the day before, to warn them of my pending inappropriate arrival.

Finally, I found the small drive in the darkness, put the car in park, and slid my bare foot off the cold, rough pedal. I searched for the number in my phone.

Deep breaths.

"Umm. Hello. I know you don't know me, and this is going to sound crazy, but I am in your driveway... and I'm naked."

Minutes later, I saw the slow, steady rising of the garage door opening, and the sweet stranger of a woman met me in the driveway and wrapped a heavy blanket around me, and we ran for cover, laughing in the rain.

Peace.

Once inside, they gave me a warm shower and a hot meal, and when I returned to the camper in the driveway for sleep, I was sure I would require a wheelchair the next day. As I fruitlessly tried to charge my dead Fitbit, my body began to violently shiver, which is exactly how it stayed until I eventually passed out in exhaustion. (One of my hiker friends later told me that he thinks I was in the early stages of hypothermia.)

The next morning, I was surprisingly fine. Apparently, my years of working out had paid off. I dried my laundry that we had put in the night before (I had to throw my sneakers away), drank a hot cup of Vermont coffee, and packed up my belongings. I said goodbye to one of the kindest, most selfless men I have ever encountered (his wife was at work) and started the next phase of my journey: New Hampshire.

Part 3
New Hampshire

Chapter Nine
Day 5, The Drive to Family

The highways in Vermont and New Hampshire are nothing like they are in Ohio. It's like you are driving aimlessly through forests and mountains, and then a random ramp appears with a sign with an exit number. Ummmm. How in the world do you know what is off the exit? Where are the gas stations? Apparently, billboards are not allowed on these highways, so you just have to know where you are going or trust that your phone is not misleading you. From highways to the Appalachian Trail, Vermont clearly doesn't like signage. It's like the whole state is set up to torment non-residents.

Along the drive, a sense of peace and joy was rising from deep within my soul. What was it about age 40 that had thrown me into a tizzy? How did I end up in this societal trap of measuring life's accomplishments by this frivolous number? Who set 40 as the magical finish line anyway? It's as if the first forty years is a giant marathon, and we have to hit so many mile markers before we cross that line into mid-life confidence and bliss.

There were mile markers, set both by myself and society, that I had missed along the way. This made me feel like I had been disqualified for the race. Instead of celebrating this great age, I felt ashamed, disappointed, and so full of regrets.

Three imperfections were the major tenets of my mid-life crisis—the dark stains upon my measurement of success:

1. My marriage had fallen apart, and I found myself unexpectedly single.

2. My figure wasn't what society, and ultimately myself, said was ideal or desirable.

3. My single-parent, teacher income was much lower than most of my friends, and I was trying to make it stretch to care for a family of three while simultaneously watching most of my friends have a more-luxurious life with their kids.

Maybe, it was the near death experience from the previous day, putting my life into perspective; maybe, it was the warmth from the kindness of strangers along my path; or maybe, it was just God quietly whispering truth, but the crust of crankiness fell off my eyes, and I began to see things differently.

Quiet Waters

For years and years of my troubling marriage, I held onto a famous Psalm in my heart, begging God to give me green pastures and quiet waters. Life was so hard, and I kept waiting for better times to come. When would He lead me to the quiet waters? Years went by, and I just kept waiting, and, eventually, I started to lose hope. All I could see was dead grass and tsunamis.

I remember sitting at my kitchen table one morning, and it hit me: it's written in present tense! "Even though I WALK", not walked. It was an epiphany. I had been waiting all this time to get out of the darkest valley when all I needed the entire time was to turn my head to see what else was there. Right next to me the whole time were green pastures and quiet waters; so many good things, like my kids, my friends, and students, were by my side. Goodness, peace, comfort, and confidence had always been there; I was just too focused on the mess to see it. God never promised the dark times would end; He just promised that the good times wouldn't end either, and it was our choice as to which way we turn our eyes.

Psalm 23 NIV Bible

The Lord is my shepherd, I lack nothing.

2

He makes me lie down in **green pastures,**

he leads me beside **quiet waters**,

3

He refreshes my soul.

He guides me along the right paths

for his name's sake.

4

Even though I walk

through the darkest valley,[a]

I will fear no evil,

for you are with me;

your rod and your staff,

they comfort me.

5

You prepare a table before me

in the presence of my enemies.

You anoint my head with oil;

my cup overflows.

6

Surely your goodness and love will follow me

all the days of my life,

and I will dwell in the house of the Lord

forever.

Now, I see myself skipping, and sometimes stumbling, on the path of life, and while there may be darkness swirling all around me as I walk, I choose to look at all the good that exists at the same time. I focus on all the blessings, and there are oh so many. Excited by this new perspective, I called up one of my best friends, Sylvia, who lives literally just across the yard from me, and she sat at my kitchen table with me that day as I shared my revelation. It was life changing.

Months after this epiphany, I was driving my way towards New Hampshire, and I began to see my life more clearly in this light. All the mile markers that I thought I had missed in life were really just doors that made room for greater goodness.

Mile Marker #1: Marriage

While true that the happily-ever-after I had envisioned when I said, "I do," was beaten to a brutal pulp, in the brokenness I found my strength, independence, and worth. I taught my children what things are not acceptable, how to stand up for themselves, how to rely on God, and ultimately how to forgive even the absolutely most atrocious of trespasses. I may have lost a dream in the destruction of my marriage, and the kids lost the "picture-perfect" family situation, but we found so much more in the healing process.

We have had a great life, truly. I don't think my boys and I would be as close as we are if we hadn't gone through these years with just the three of us. We fiercely love, respect, support and protect each other. And we are friends. We have a flow, and we are comfortable. Our space is full of peace, love, and laughter, and I know, without a shadow of doubt, God made our life after divorce even better than it would have been had I stayed in a bad marriage.

For years while tucking my kids in their beds, I have bragged to them, "I know I'm God's favorite...because he gave me you." I mean it to my very core.

Missed mile marker #1, debunked.

Mile marker #2: Weight

Look, I spent years of my life thinking I was fat when I wasn't. Never in my childhood was I ever teased or even acknowledged as fat, other than a rude and seemingly weight-obsessed pediatrician and my own inner voices of insecurity. It wasn't until returning to America after an extended trip doing medical clinics in Africa that my weight began to soar. I had caught some kind of terrible rash that had taken over my body, and no doctor could identify it. The itching was so intense that I literally began ripping the skin off of my body. After countless tests from various doctors, it was discovered that only an extremely high dose of the steroid Prednisone would tame the evil bumps. So, I lived on this drug for nearly two years, packing on 60 pounds in total. After that, I bore two children, and to this day I battle with the bulge.

Now, this isn't to say I wasn't always meatier in certain places, like my thighs and upper arms. When I was 19, I remember sitting crisscross applesauce on my boyfriend's bed. He grabbed an inner thigh in each one of his hands, began shaking them and said, "problem area?"

Hurt, I immediately grabbed his genital region in my hand, began shaking and replied, "problem area?"

But despite this isolated incident of stupidity, my weight was only an issue in my own head. In fact, my weight insecurities led me to a life of good health and, ultimately, a life full of good friends and joy. Looking back, I can see how many dear friends I have bonded and laughed with through acts of exercise. Very few of my friends have not hit a trail, a workout class, or participated on a sports team with me because exercise has always been such a part of my active lifestyle.

So, what appeared to be another missed marker, in fact, was one of the greatest developers in what I like about my life today. I may not be everyone's cup of tea in terms of body type, but the truth is, not everyone is mine either. We all have physical preferences in others, and that's okay. I'm actually glad I have something about me that isn't favored by some people because this helps me narrow my search. Eliminating what I don't like, and those that don't like me (there are plenty that do), is quite handy in this proverbial sea of love possibilities. I've learned in my countless dating horrors that most men don't even mind a heavier woman; all that really matters is confidence and how you carry yourself.

Missed mile marker #2, debunked.

Mile marker #3: Finances

There were days I'd throw aprons on the boys and myself and challenge them to an in-home episode of Chopped. We'd scrounge the kitchen for any ingredients to possibly make an edible meal. Little did they know that on these days this was the best I could do to provide because there was no money left for groceries. Instead of sadness and pity, we had ingenuity and laughter.

This is only one of countless ways lacking money brought about goodness in our lives. It taught me to budget, be creative, say no, and appreciate what I have and what is given to me.

In addition, my kids and I have never gone without a roof over our heads. When I first became divorced, I had just started a new career path: teaching. Unable to secure a public school job due to an English teacher hiring freeze in Columbus, I took my master's degree and teaching license and secured a high school teaching job at a Christian school with the staggering annual salary of $21,000. Yes, that was in 2012.

In order to manage to continue to live in our own home, I picked up two side jobs. I taught a freshman English class at my undergraduate alma mater, Capital University. I'd teach high school all day long, and my best friend would pick up my little kids (ages 2 ½ and 5 when this started) for me while I ran to the university to teach a class. Then, I'd run home to feed and bathe my kids. Once they were in bed, I would hop online to complete my third job: editing textbooks for Pearson Education.

This went on for a couple years until I finally made my way into the public school system, which offered a slightly better pay and enabled me to eventually only have to work one job.

Here's the thing, due to my emergency-level need for money as a newly single parent with a late-start career, I was forced to follow one of my greatest dreams of being a professor. It was beyond fulfilling to work alongside the very professors that taught me years ago when I first attended college. To be honest, it was also a dream to be in a position to actually hear myself being called "Professor" by my students. If it weren't for the lack of money in my life, I never would have experienced this dream come true.

If this isn't exciting enough on its own, there has been an even greater blessing I found in my lack of financial abundance. After the demise of my marriage, I found myself alone in the state of Ohio with no family, trying to raise two boys, one of whom was still in diapers. I couldn't keep up with my house, yard, driveway, children, and three jobs (mental sanity wasn't even an option at the time), and I needed to find a new place for us to live.

I was talking to a good friend of mine from my church about all that had gone down, and he told me to pick a house, and he would pay cash for it, saying I could pay him back for it. What?! Who says that?! My first instinct was to reject the offer, being way too great. Ultimately, I agreed, knowing there would be no other way for me to get a house at this time since my husband and I had temporarily ruined our credit by short-selling our previous home.

Seriously though, who has friends that do this kind of thing? And who has friends that can even afford such a thing? This friend owned his own law firm and had a successful realty business on the side. He had the ability to do this kind thing for me and told me he wouldn't do it for anyone but me, saying he knew my character and knew I wouldn't take advantage.

So I bought a small condo, knowing it would be easier to juggle so many things without having to worry about a yard and snow shoveling, and when we went to sign the title, my friend kept joking that I was his mistress. You know everyone was wondering, but it was far from the truth. He and his wife were both treasured friends of mine, and such a thing couldn't have been any further from the truth. But still, I blushed. We laughed and offered no explanation, because it was none of their business.

A year later, when my credit was restored, I refinanced with a proper loan from a bank, making sure my dear friend received interest on the 12 months for which he funded my loan.

This three-bedroom condo with a fully finished basement has been, and still is, a single-mother sanctuary. The neighborhood park is literally in our front yard, and on snowy and rainy days, all the kids pile into our basement, known as the Kid Cave. The three of us couldn't be happier.

It looks like the expectation of perceived needed finances I had was also a fraud.

Missed mile marker 3, debunked.

So, it turns out I did complete the race; the mile markers just didn't look like I thought they would. I had set markers based on how I interpreted success in our society, but "missing" these marks actually set me free into deeper areas of other successes. From these areas of lack, I gained creativity, authenticity, ingenuity, connection, confidence, independence, and so much more. I wasn't disqualified from the race; I nailed it–and then some.

These were the thoughts running through my now relaxed mind when my GPS bellowed, "Arrived," and I slowly pulled by rental car into my relatives' (yet still strangers) driveway.

Chapter Ten
Day 5 Continued, Relatives

So, how did this crisis trip end up in New Hampshire? At some point prior tothis journey, I saw a post by my beloved cousin that she and my uncle were up in Boston, a long way from their Florida residence. I reached out to her and found they were staying with another uncle of ours in New Hampshire. Now, I've never really known either of these uncles, especially the one in New Hampshire, so I basically invited myself to join their party, to which they politely obliged.

My mother and her siblings are 100% Italian, but I've never really learned anything about my family and heritage from her. Both her parents were dead before I was born, and I was raised in a different state from where the majority of our relatives resided. I've always longed to know about my Italian family, so I basically spent the next two days drinking red wine, eating cheese, and swapping stories with my beloved relatives. I felt like I had found my people.

I was feeling quite emotional when it came time for me to leave. We had driven to a diner for a large breakfast, and from there I would drive back to Boston for the night and catch my flight home the following morning. Tears streamed down my face when I had to say goodbye to my Uncle Billy and Aunt Ridie, whom I felt I had just begun to know, fully aware I may never make it back to see them again.

Chapter Eleven
Day 7, Back to Boston

After leaving my relatives and settling into my stupidly expensive room near the Boston airport, I stationed myself with my journal and a bottle of red wine in the hotel restaurant. It was here I scribbled the last of my journey notes, relishing in the final moments of my adventure.

About halfway through my bottle, I struck up a conversation with the couple sitting at the table next to me, who had apparently been wondering if I was writing a book. I shared with them the highlights of my trip and the reason behind it, and the woman began telling me about her own navigation through a life crisis. She was a realtor, and he was a pilot for the airline I was using the next day. This was the beginning of a friendship that still lasts today.

The next morning, I caught a mid-morning flight back home with a deep peace within my soul and a new perspective in my pocket.

An update in the form of an Epic List Poem

Some months have passed since my crisis journey ended, and I have to be honest and report that one of the issues I tackled, unsuccessful love relationships, has attempted to still rear its ugly head a few times. It turns out that finding yourself on a wild adventure is not a one-and-done type of self-awareness arrival. The journey continues, but this time I am different. I'm stronger, clearer, and can feel it in my cracking bones. When I start to lose my head in the present, I remind myself of my past and find myself again (no need for a near death experience to reflect now), knowing the future is yet to be explored, celebrated, and devoured. I'm ready for every last bite.

So, here's to doing better and being better, my loves. And when you find yourself lost in the woods, in the cold and stormy rain, and feel like no hope is to be found, just know that the warmth is coming. You WILL find the road to the rental car. Just…keep…crawling.

Part One: What I Have Done

I have…
Skinny dipped under the stars countless times
in water that had no business
sharing space with my private parts.
Stolen my parents' car for joy rides
well before driving age
and anyone teaching me how to drive.
Swam competitively, both race and synchronized,
And won last place in district diving championship.
Earned with the most graceful frog position
Sailing through the air.
Someone had to lose.
Won a disco dancing contest
In front of my entire high school.
The prize was a giant Hershey bar
that I'm pretty sure I never ate.
Learned to play saxophone,
Piano,
And to sing a mediocre tune.

*

I have…
Ballroom danced on a mountaintop in Austria
While the night sky stormed.
Made love to my husband (now ex) in a tent
In the middle of the Amazon Jungle.
Been bitten by a piranha
While bathing in the Amazon River.

He took a chunk right out of my foot,

Forcing me to rise up like Jesus,

Running on water for the riverbank.

Traveled to Colombia, Peru, and Brazil, twice,

Bringing water purifiers and dental care

To tribes in the most polluted portions of the Amazon.

Ran the streets of Bogota by myself,

Knowing no Spanish,

Until I bartered a ticket to the jungle,

In search of a team that I never met and had left me behind.

Studied the secret police

And Martin Luther

One summer in Germany.

Walked the sacred ground of a concentration camp,

Buchenwald,

Weeping at the rooms full of dead kids' shoes

And the human-sized brick ovens.

Been kicked out of China

For smuggling Bibles across the border

In fat suits, pregnant suits, and business trolleys.

Rode across China in a sleeper bus and train,

While cockroaches crawled across my face,

And government soldiers slept beside me,

Unaware of the contraband in my luggage.

Delivered Bibles to the Underground Church

In dark hotel rooms in the middle of the night.

Washing their feet with the water in a hotel wastebasket,

And them washing mine.

Eaten meals prepared for me on coffee cans as a stove

In humble homes no bigger than my bedroom closet,

Deep within the rivers and mountains of Guilin.

Built orphanages in Mexico

While the sweet angels watched in curiosity.

Mourned the separation of my homeland

with strangers in rural England

When I was emergency grounded

While attempting to fly back to America

from Ireland

On 9/11.

Walked among Kings,

Even was proposed to by one,

While studying the Kanuri tribe

And doing medical clinics

In Cameroon and Nigeria.

Purchased peanuts and coconut sweet

Off the heads of children working the markets

On the very shores that still mourn the loss of ancestors

Stolen in the slave trade.

Stood at the foot of a dock that barely still stands,

And was the last step of so many feet

As they were ripped from their African homes.

Visited Ireland twice to meet my nieces,

Born to my brother and his wife,

As they dedicated their lives to get drug-addicted kids

Off the streets of Belfast.

Eaten a proper Irish breakfast,

Actually in Ireland,

And lunched on Bangers and Mash.

*

I have…

Eaten a pear while staring head on into my BFFs vagina,

As she pushed out my first godson

And his impressively large head,

Without meds,

Yet I was the one that passed out and needed sugar.

Felt life grow inside me.

Had my body cut open,

Moved around,

Welded, and stapled back together again.

Lost two babies:

One in secret

And one in a toilet

On the main floor bathroom

Next to the kitchen.

I still can hear my screams.

Her birthday would have been the 4th of July.

Gave birth to a rainbow baby,

Whose name means strength, and

I thank God for his survival.

Earned a master's degree and a teaching license,

Graduating with a 4.0 while

Simultaneously raising a 2-month old and 2-year old,

Running a full-time daycare out of my home,

and dealing with a troubled marriage.

Became a professor and taught

Alongside the same professors that taught me years before.

Worked three jobs to pay the bills as a single mom:

High school teacher by day,

College Professor by late afternoon,

Online textbook editor by night

After my babies were in bed.

Juggled all this with full custody

And not a single blood-relative

Living in my entire state.

Gained and lost so many pounds in this life

That it is impossible to track.

Published poetry

And articles about the persecuted church around the world,

Well before I met their members.

I've faced the day strong,

Smiling and focused,

Even when I was dying inside.

Survived hate crimes in the form of a bomb in my mailbox,

As my husband and children were the only non-whites

In an otherwise all white, suburban neighborhood.

We survived trucks running us off the road,

People dumping trash on us on a walk, and

Church folk leaving the church

Because our marriage was "against God," and

White folks protesting in the form of refusing to eat

In the same restaurant room as me and my black husband.

Drove The Four Tops

Through a White Castle drive-thru

And Peter, Paul, and Mary to a golf course in Columbus.

Purchased coffee for Burt Bacharach,

Out of my own nearly empty pockets,

From the Coffee Beanery

In the mall formerly known as The City Center.

Purchased my own homes,

Three times.

Travelled many parts of America

with just me and my two sons

And a playlist of smooth jams.

And, of course, now I can say

That I hiked the Appalachian Trail,

By myself,

With nothing but a toddler backpack

And Jesus.

Part Two: What I Am

Kind

Patient

Courageous

Spontaneous

Bold

Transparent

Empathetic

Strong

Resilient

Confident

Intelligent

Optimistic

Creative

Helpful

Happy

Silly

Independent

Loving

Generous

Giving

A fighter for justice,

a voice for the liberation of others,

And now a voice fighting for my own.

Part Three: What I Am Not

The dirt beneath the sole of your shoes.

Epilogue
Darkest Brown #4

Weeks have passed since my own gray roots started to resurface. Life has a way of filling up the hours of the day, and beautification sometimes falls by the wayside.

But tonight is the night. I have a two-hour window without my boys, so I crack open a box of Darkest Brown #4.

In my haste, I put on the oversized, clear plastic gloves and mix up the chemicals without even reading the directions. Directions are for people that care too much. Those gray traitors aren't worth ten extra seconds of my time. I'm a mad cosmetological scientist, taking the fate of my betraying head of hair into my own hands.

I've been told the people in my family gray early. My second cousin, Paula, supposedly had a full head of gray hair by age thirteen, and I remembered being horrified to learn that her mother, as the story goes, wouldn't let her dye it. Can you imagine having to endure your entire high school career with a head full of granny hair?

Unlike my cousin, I didn't start to turn gray until my late twenties—until I was pregnant, to be exact—, and I only have a halo of gray hair that basically outlines my face—old lady edges. They are prominent and wiry and basically announce to the world that I'm older than I try to appear. Humanity has no business knowing this truth. It is mine, and my business only, to share if I so choose. Those gray hairs are overstepping their boundaries, and they must pay.

"You'll understand one day," I hear my mother's ancient voice re-emerge.

Without care, I start squirting bursts of revenge on the natural part in my hair, recklessly rubbing it into my scalp. I do zero preparation to my face to avoid staining my skin, and I haphazardly part my hair every so many centimeters and repeat the violent squirting and rubbing of the dye.

Within minutes, I slathered my hair in a healthy concentration of the chemicals, and I looked down to see that I had victimized the white porcelain sink with dark brown legions in the process. I drop a dye-colored glove on the floor and attempt to wipe yet another stain off of the floor. Gloveless, I begin to feverishly rub the dye out of the sink with some wet toilet paper and hand soap, but the darkness doesn't budge. All that I accomplish is a silver dollar-sized brown stain now upon my hand.

I clean up the mess of the bathroom, set the timer on my phone for twenty minutes, and proceed to fold laundry. Upon my return to the bathroom, I glanced in the mirror and was immediately taken aback.

"Oh my. This isn't good."

In attempting to rub out all the naughty gray edges upon my head, apparently I instead gave my skin a half-inch edge of Darkest Brown #4. I tried everything to erase it. Hot water. Soap. Toothpaste. Desperate bargaining with God.

No luck.

"*We're on our way back*," the text reads from my best friend. Within minutes, my kids would be home, and I looked like I'd taken a chocolate brown Sharpie to my face.

I warned my bestie with a humorous text. When she arrived, we investigated my hairline together in the downstairs bathroom, my forehead just inches from her eyeballs, as I hunched over her as she peed.

"Oh well. It's not that bad if I keep my hair down," I shrugged.

We laughed.